The
SHADOW WORK
JOURNAL

ALSO BY KEILA SHAHEEN

The Vibrational Poetry Book

The 369 Journal, Limitless Edition

The Lucky Girl Journal

The
SHADOW WORK
JOURNAL

SECOND EDITION

A Guide to Integrate and Transcend Your Shadows

Keila Shaheen

PRIMERO
SUEÑO PRESS

ATRIA

New York London Toronto Sydney New Delhi

**PRIMERO
SUEÑO PRESS**

ATRIA

An Imprint of Simon & Schuster, LLC
1230 Avenue of the Americas
New York, NY 10020

This Primero Sueño Press/Atria Paperback edition April 2024

PRIMERO SUEÑO PRESS **/ ATRIA** PAPERBACK and colophon are trademarks
of Simon & Schuster, LLC

Simon & Schuster: Celebrating 100 Years of Publishing in 2024

For information about special discounts for bulk purchases, please contact Simon & Schuster Special Sales at 1-866-506-1949 or business@simonandschuster.com.

The Simon & Schuster Speakers Bureau can bring authors to your live event. For more information or to book an event, contact the Simon & Schuster Speakers Bureau at 1-866-248-3049 or visit our website at www.simonspeakers.com.

Interior design by Nicole Tereza

Manufactured in the United States of America

1   3   5   7   9   10   8   6   4   2

ISBN 978-1-6680-6918-9
ISBN 978-1-6680-7051-2 (ebook)

DOWNLOAD
the APP

Scan Here

WHERE TECHNOLOGY MEETS
INNER TRANSFORMATION

- Track Triggers

- Check In with Feelings

- Journal Prompts

- Healing Exercises

- View Emotional Patterns over Time

DECLARATION
of INTENT

I,_____, vow on this day to commit
to my personal growth and acceptance. I promise to fill this journal
out with an open heart and good intentions. I acknowledge that
there are both pure and wounded parts to my being, and I choose
to embrace and nurture both. I look forward to unveiling my shadows
and bringing more light into this world through my personal journey
of self-reflection and healing.

_____

SIGNATURE

_____

START DATE

_____

COMPLETION DATE

DEAR READER,

I am Keila Shaheen, the creator of this journal and your companion on this transformative journey. As you hold this journal, know that we are kindred spirits, united in our quest for inner growth, seeking to understand ourselves and the world more deeply.

Like many, I've navigated life trying to fit in, often feeling out of place. Stepping into the corporate environment after COVID, I encountered intense social anxiety and felt deeply disconnected from others, a reflection of my own inner disconnection. I thrived in one-on-one interactions but found myself lost in group settings, my thoughts racing yet unspoken. It was during these challenging times that I turned to the one constant in my life: my journal.

The term "shadow work" came to me serendipitously as I explored ways to heal and understand myself. Carl Jung's concept resonated deeply, giving a name and structure to the introspective work I had been doing. This journal, which began as a personal sanctuary, transformed into a mission: to share the power of shadow work with the world. This transformation led to my creation of Zenfulnote, a platform dedicated to guiding others on their journey of self-discovery and holistic well-being.

I have recognized that in this era of rapid change and deep questioning, humanity finds itself at a crossroads, yearning for a profound message that connects our innermost selves with the vast mysteries of the universe. We are no longer content with surface-level explanations and are instead drawn to explore the deeper meaning of our existence. By engaging in this introspective practice, we not only gain insight into our personal psyche but also tap into the collective wisdom that has guided humanity for generations. This process of exploration and discovery is not just a path to personal enlightenment but also a step toward a more profound, collective understanding of the human experience in its entirety. In essence, this journal is a bridge between the individual and the universal.

For me, shadow work is an openhearted journey into the self. It's about peeling back the layers of our psyche to reveal our hidden fears, desires, and truths. It's a process of embracing our humanity— our imperfections, vulnerabilities, and strengths. Through this practice, I found my purpose, my voice, and a profound sense of wholeness. It has taught me the value of self-awareness and compassion, not just for myself but for the world around me. This *Shadow Work Journal* is a culmination of that journey and the beginning of yours. With more than a million copies sold in the United States alone, and versions being published in at least twenty-seven countries around the world, this journal has touched countless lives. For me, its impact has been far-reaching and deeply humbling. As you venture into these pages, my hope is that you find in them a mirror for your soul, a space to confront and embrace your shadows, and a guide to living a life that is fully and authentically yours.

Welcome to your journey of shadow work. May it be as enlightening, transformative, and healing for you as it has been for me.

With love,
Keila Shaheen

PARTS

Contents

3. INTEGRATE YOUR SHADOW EXERCISES

4. JOURNAL PROMPTS

5. GET TO THE ROOT

"UNLESS YOU LEARN TO FACE YOUR OWN
SHADOWS, YOU WILL CONTINUE TO SEE
THEM IN OTHERS, BECAUSE THE WORLD
OUTSIDE OF YOU IS ONLY A REFLECTION
OF THE WORLD INSIDE YOU."

—CARL JUNG

1

Shadow Work
Introduction

What Is Shadow Work?

Shadow work is about revealing the unknown. The shadow is an unconscious aspect of your personality that the ego does not identify with. You might experience your shadow when it's triggered in social interactions, relationships, and in episodes of anxiety or sadness.

The unconscious mind contains repressed emotions from painful events, causing impulsive behaviors and unwanted patterns that form your "dark side." In short, the shadow is composed of the parts of yourself that you have forgotten, abandoned, and repressed in order to grow and fit in with the constructs of society. Think back to your childhood and recall the ways in which you would express yourself only to be rejected. You may have been crying and told to stop. You may have been laughing uncontrollably in a classroom and given a dirty glance from your teacher or peers.

There are countless ways in which you may have been reprimanded for what was deemed "bad" and praised for what was "good"—learning to adjust your behavior accordingly. These repressed parts of yourself don't go away forever. They are stored and locked inside your unconscious mind. Shadow work is the process of revealing, accepting, and integrating these parts of yourself that you have repressed and rejected. The techniques in *The Shadow Work Journal* will allow you to dive into unconscious pockets of repressed emotions and transcend the negative effects they currently have on your well-being.

> *The goal is to make the unconscious conscious so that you may work on these emotions in self-reflection and acceptance. While anyone can do shadow work, a licensed mental health expert is a good option, especially for individuals who have experienced severe trauma or abuse.*

Before beginning your shadow work, it is important to set an intention to openly notice and question your own reactions. The shadow is apparent in strong emotions and dissatisfaction. Be sure to keep a mental log of these sensations to truly understand where patterns occur, and use this journal as a tool to identify what is causing them. The "Getting to the Root of Your Shadow" pages are an excellent resource to track your shadows and their origins.

Why Shadow Work Is Important

There are many benefits to shadow work. Your pains and triggers can be guides to help you understand what you deeply care about, bringing you closer to your life purpose. Conversely, you will come to identify toxic patterns in your life and change them completely.

Another benefit of shadow work is that you will develop more courage and confidence to face the unknown and embody your whole self.

You will develop deeper love, acceptance, and understanding of yourself, which helps improve your relationships with others. Practicing shadow work helps you separate from your egotistical thoughts and will increase your empathy and compassion for others. Compassion, in turn, helps exercise other forms of positive emotions like gratitude, which can better your mental and physical health.

Failure to face and deal with the shadow elements can be the seed of adversities and prejudice between unrepresented groups or individuals, and can trigger anything from a small argument to a major war. Recognizing shadow elements is an integral part of becoming a compassionate and reasonable individual.

The Father of Shadow Work: Carl Jung

The concept of the shadow was first developed by Swiss psychiatrist and psychoanalyst Carl Jung. Jung believed that exploring the shadow was essential for personal growth and individuation, the process of becoming one's authentic self. The shadow refers to the unconscious parts of our psyche that contain our repressed thoughts, feelings, and impulses. It is the side of ourselves that we reject or hide from others, and often from ourselves. However, these repressed aspects of ourselves can still influence our behavior and emotional states.

Understanding the Psyche

The "psyche" is a term used to describe the inner world of our thoughts, feelings, and emotions. It is the source of our experiences, motivations, and behaviors, and it is constantly evolving and changing throughout our lives. Understanding the psyche is key to understanding ourselves and the world around us.

> *Jung believed that the psyche was composed of several distinct but interrelated parts, including the conscious mind and the unconscious mind, made up of the personal unconscious and the collective unconscious.*

The conscious mind (the ego) is the part of our psyche that is aware of our thoughts and experiences. The unconscious mind contains thoughts, feelings, and experiences that are outside our awareness. The personal unconscious is the part of the psyche that contains repressed thoughts, feelings, and experiences, while the collective unconscious is the part of the psyche that contains archetypes and universal symbols and themes that are shared by all people. One of the key benefits of understanding the psyche is increased self-awareness. When we have a greater understanding of our thoughts, feelings, and emotions, we can make more conscious choices, improve our relationships with others, and reduce anxiety and emotional distress.

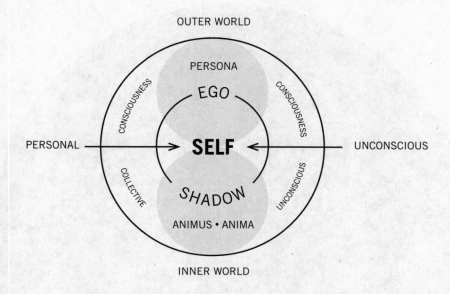

Figure 1: Jung's model of the psyche

Jung believed that exploring the psyche was essential for personal growth and individuation, the process of becoming one's authentic self. He believed that by exploring the unconscious mind, we could gain a deeper understanding of our motivations, reactions, and behaviors, and make changes to live more authentic lives. Jung's theories, building on the foundational work of his mentor Sigmund Freud, have significantly influenced the field of psychology, inspiring subsequent generations of psychoanalytic theorists to further develop and diversify these concepts. Today, the study of the psyche is an interdisciplinary field that draws on psychology, neuroscience, philosophy, and spirituality.

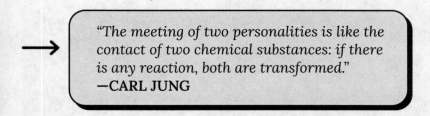

"The meeting of two personalities is like the contact of two chemical substances: if there is any reaction, both are transformed."
—CARL JUNG

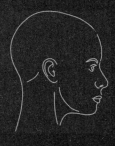

MIND TRAPS

ANCHORING
The first thing you judge
influences your judgment
of all that follows.

CONFIRMATION BIAS
You favor things that confirm
your existing beliefs.

REACTANCE
You'd rather do the opposite
of what someone is trying
to make you do.

**SUNK COST
FALLACY**
You irrationally cling to
things that have already
cost you something.

**DUNNING-
KRUGER EFFECT**
The more you know, the less
confident you are likely to be.

**BACKFIRE
EFFECT**
When your core beliefs
are challenged, it can
cause you to believe in
them more strongly.

DECLINISM
You remember the past
better than it was,
and expect the future
to be worse than
it will likely be.

**FRAMING
EFFECT**
You allow yourself to be
influenced by context
and delivery.

**NEGATIVITY
BIAS**
You allow negative things
to disproportionately
influence your thinking.

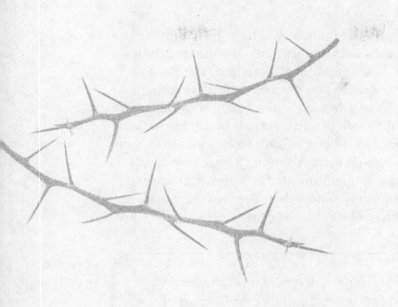

How to Do Shadow Work

Shadow work involves exploring the unconscious aspects of ourselves in a safe and controlled environment. This can include journaling, meditation, therapy, or working with a spiritual teacher or guide (*The Shadow Work Journal* can serve as your guide). The goal of shadow work is to bring the unconscious into consciousness and integrate it into our lives. By doing this, we can gain a greater understanding of our motivations, reactions, and behaviors, and make changes to live more authentic lives. We all have multiple parts to ourselves, and if we don't embrace the entirety of our being, we won't be able to live a whole and authentic life. The process of integrating the shadow leads to self-acceptance, forgiveness, and unconditional love.

In order to flush out your shadow, you must be willing to catch yourself in moments of negativity and question where they stem from. Use this journal's "Getting to the Root of Your Shadow" pages when you notice yourself becoming irritated, anxious, angry, or sad. When facing your shadow, it is important to take small positive actions that improve your physical and mental well-being. Drink more water than you think you need, dress up more, shower, cleanse your face, eat something light and healthy, do breathing exercises, or listen to music you enjoy. Know that the discomfort will pass and you will feel like yourself again.

→ *"Knowing your own darkness is the best method for dealing with the darknesses of other people."* —CARL JUNG

The shadow carries all the things we do not want to know about ourselves or do not like. While difficult and painful, it is important that we work at owning our shadow to bring it into a relationship with our consciousness. Owning up to our shadow is an important part of self-awareness and healing. As you go through *The Shadow Work Journal*, remember to show those parts of yourself unconditional love.

The Mindset: Self-Compassion

One of the key aspects of shadow work is self-compassion.
When you begin to explore the shadow, it can be challenging
to face the parts of yourself that you reject or hide. It is
important to approach shadow work with a nonjudgmental
attitude and to treat yourself with the same kindness and
compassion that you would offer a friend. By doing this, you
can create a safe and supportive environment for exploration
and growth. Self-compassion involves recognizing and
accepting our own human limitations, failures, and experiences
of suffering, rather than harsh self-criticism and judgment.

Our culture often emphasizes perfectionism and individual achievement, which can lead to feelings of inadequacy and self-criticism when we fall short.

Self-compassion is the foundation of a meaningful life, for it is only through the lens of kindness and understanding toward ourselves that we truly can see and accept others.

The Importance of Grounding

Another important aspect of shadow work is grounding. Grounding is a technique that helps to anchor us in the present moment, to connect with our bodies, and to find stability and balance in a chaotic world. It helps to reduce stress and anxiety by bringing us out of our heads and into the now. Shadow work can be intense and emotionally challenging, and it is important to take steps to ensure that you are in a safe and stable state of mind before and after the process. This can include meditation, deep breathing, or other practices that help you feel centered and grounded. Whenever you need it, flip to the Release Stagnant Energy exercise on page 50 for a few options to help you ground.

It is important to ground yourself before and after using *The Shadow Work Journal.*

Here are a few ways to easily ground yourself:

1. **Simple Recognition**
   Recognize common humanity: Remember that everyone experiences setbacks, failures, and moments of suffering. You are not alone, and your experiences are a normal part of the human experience.

2. **Self-care**
   Engage in activities that bring you joy, relaxation, and a sense of well-being. This can include things like exercise, hobbies, spending time with loved ones, and getting enough sleep.

3. **Affirmations**
   Using positive affirmations can help to reduce stress and increase feelings of well-being.

4. **Sensory Stimulation**
   Engaging our senses through activities such as walking in nature, smelling essential oils, or eating a nourishing meal can help to bring us into the present moment.

5. **Deep Breathing**
   Taking slow, deep breaths can help to calm the mind and reduce stress.

How to Spot Your Shadow Self

Spotting your shadow self often begins with noticing your triggers, recognizing patterns in your behavior and life experiences, and understanding your projections.

1. **Noticing Your Triggers**
   Triggers produce emotional responses that are often intense and seemingly disproportionate to the situation at hand. They are indicators that a part of you, often a shadow aspect, feels threatened or hurt. When you're triggered, it can feel as if you're reacting automatically, without a conscious choice. These triggers are valuable clues, pointing toward your underlying unresolved issues or "shadows." To spot your triggers, take a step back and objectively look at situations that cause you to react intensely. Is there a common theme or factor? It could be a word, an action, a type of person, or even a place that repeatedly causes an emotional upheaval in you.

2. **Recognizing Patterns**
   The patterns we're looking for here are repetitive behaviors that may not serve you but seem hard to break free from. They often manifest in your relationships, choices, reactions, or habits. These patterns can be a sign of a shadow self that's trying to make its presence felt. Recognizing these patterns involves self-reflection. Consider the common threads in your past experiences, relationships, and reactions. Are you repeatedly drawn to similar types of relationships or situations, only to experience the same negative outcomes? Do you often react in the same way, even when you wish you didn't? These repetitive patterns might indicate areas where shadow work can be beneficial.

3. Understanding Projections

Projections are aspects of ourselves that we unconsciously place onto others. These can be qualities that we both admire and detest. When we have a strong emotional reaction to someone else's behavior or qualities, it often signifies a disowned part of ourselves—a shadow aspect.

To understand your projections, consider the characteristics in others that you find extremely irritating or, conversely, overly admire. Then, ask yourself if these traits could be parts of yourself that you've disowned or idealized.

4. Pay Attention to Dreams

Your dreams are a rich source of symbolism, an unconscious vault. Try to recall and record your dreams upon waking up. Analyze the symbols, emotions, and themes present in your dreams. They can provide valuable insights into your shadows, fears, desires, and unexpressed parts of yourself.

5. Explore Childhood and Past Experiences

Reflect on your childhood, family dynamics, and significant life events. Identify any unresolved issues, traumas, or unmet needs that might have contributed to the development of your shadows. Exploring these experiences with compassion and curiosity can lead to profound healing and integration.

Here Are Three Signs That It's Time to Work with a Professional

1. **Overwhelming Emotions**
   If you're consistently feeling overwhelmed, anxious, or depressed and it's negatively impacting your daily life, it might be time to seek professional help.

2. **Recurring Dreams or Nightmares**
   Persistent, distressing dreams can indicate unresolved issues in your unconscious. A mental health professional can not only help decode, but also help you work through these issues.

3. **Social Withdrawal**
   If you find yourself pulling away from loved ones, avoiding social events, or feeling isolated, it could be a sign that you need support in navigating your inner world.

Working with a professional can be incredibly helpful and is really recommended when engaging in this deeper type of healing, if you need a little support as you begin your work around uncovering.

Interested in Doing Shadow Work with a Therapist?

Therapist Green Flags

1. They are clear about their scope of practice (and their limitations).

2. They ask questions that allow you to reflect on yourself within lived experience.

3. They establish safety first and earn trust gradually.

4. They check in on you and your progress throughout the experience.

5. They teach you about emotional dysregulation and regulation.

6. They gently present new response and reaction options.

7. You feel seen and heard with them.

Integrating Your Shadow Self

Emotional freedom technique (EFT) tapping is a powerful therapeutic tool that combines elements of cognitive therapy and acupressure. It can be a valuable method for integrating your shadow self and facilitating deep emotional healing. By combining specific tapping sequences on meridian points with focused attention on unresolved emotions and beliefs, EFT can help release energetic blockages, promote self-acceptance, and facilitate the integration of shadow aspects. Later in *The Shadow Work Journal*, we will explore how to use EFT tapping as a means of integrating your shadow self and promoting holistic healing.

To begin EFT tapping, identify the shadow aspects you wish to integrate. Reflect on the emotions, beliefs, or memories that arise when you think about these aspects. You will also want to familiarize yourself with the basic tapping points used in EFT. These points include the top of the head, the eyebrow, the side of the eye, under the eye, under the nose, the chin, the collarbone, and under the arm. Gently tap each point with two or three fingers while repeating a relevant statement or focusing on the associated emotion.

Another technique is to use inner-child affirmations. Craft affirmations that specifically address the shadows you have identified. Affirmations should be present-tense statements that reflect self-acceptance, healing, and integration.

Ongoing awareness is a powerful tool for integrating shadows and promoting personal growth. By becoming a "butterfly net" for your triggers and negative thoughts, you can actively engage in identifying, understanding, and integrating your shadows. This practice cultivates self-awareness, empowers you to respond consciously, and opens the door to transformation and healing.

Understanding Emotional Triggers

Shame

Shame is an intense emotion that arises when you believe
there is something fundamentally wrong with who you are.
It is a deeply painful and isolating experience that can stem
from feeling unworthy, inadequate, or humiliated. Shame can
manifest as a heavy burden that weighs us down, making us feel
small and undeserving of love and acceptance. It often arises
from societal expectations, past traumas, or internalized beliefs.
Overcoming shame requires compassion, self-acceptance, and a
recognition of our inherent worthiness as human beings.

Guilt

Guilt arises when we believe we have done something wrong or
violated our own moral code. It's a form of self-condemnation and
blame, mixed with a sense of regret. Guilt can be a constructive
emotion, because it reveals your values and helps you learn from
mistakes. It signals a need for accountability and encourages us to
make amends or change our behavior. When left unchecked, guilt
can transform into an overwhelming burden, leading to excessive
self-criticism and preventing personal growth.

Anger

Anger is a powerful and complex emotion that is spurred in
response to perceived threats, injustice, or frustration. It can range
from mild to intense and can manifest as a physical or emotional
response. Anger is a natural and valid emotion that reveals a need
for change or boundaries. Uncontrolled or excessive anger can
lead to destructive behavior and harm to oneself and others.

Sadness

Sadness is a deep and poignant emotion that arises in response
to loss, disappointment, or unfulfilled desires. Sadness can be
triggered by a variety of experiences such as the loss of a loved
one, the end of a relationship, or unmet expectations. It is a
natural and necessary part of the human experience.

Embarrassment
This emotion stems from feeling self-conscious, awkward, or humiliated in social situations. It often happens when you think you have violated social norms. Ongoing embarrassment can lead to feeling shame and a desire to hide.

Jealousy
Jealousy is a cover-up emotion. It masks itself as anger or judgment, when underneath it's sadness and dissatisfaction with the self. It can lead you to compare yourself to others, and protect what you have.

Regret
Regret occurs when you feel sadness over past actions or decisions. The truth is that most people regret what they did not do more than they regret what they did do.

Fear
Fear is a primal and powerful emotion that arises in response to perceived threats or dangers. It triggers a domino of physiological and emotional responses to keep you "safe." Fear can serve as a protective mechanism, but irrational fear can limit our experiences and growth. Overcoming fear involves understanding its root causes, challenging irrational beliefs, and gradually exposing yourself to feared situations in a safe and supportive manner.

> *The journey of self-discovery requires the willingness to explore the depths of our shadows and the heights of our potential.*

"THE PRIVILEGE OF A LIFETIME IS TO BECOME WHO YOU TRULY ARE."

—CARL JUNG

_____

Decompressing after Shadow Work

Our compassionate Zenfulnote therapists have shared their pearls of wisdom to guide you in gently decompressing after your journey into the self.

Tip #1: Embrace Gentle Movement
Reconnect with the rhythm of your body through gentle, nurturing activities. Our therapists recommend yoga or tranquil walks in the embrace of nature. These are not mere physical exercises; they are rituals of release and rejuvenation. As you move, imagine the physical and emotional tensions melting away, leaving you refreshed and realigned.

Tip #2: Honor Your Unique Needs
Decompression is as individual as your journey. What is your inner voice calling for? It might be the reflective practice of journaling, the energy-releasing power of exercise, or the quietude of a personal retreat. This is a time to prioritize and honor your well-being, embracing practices that resonate with your deepest needs.

Tip #3: Find Solace in Creativity
After shadow work, creativity can be a powerful ally. Immerse yourself in creative pursuits that light up your spirit. Whether it's through painting, music, baking, or any other form of art, let these activities be a conduit for your emotions. There's profound healing and understanding to be found in every creative act that fulfills your deepest needs.

Cherishing Your Journey

As you tread this transformative path, remember that the act of decompressing is as significant as the journey itself. It's in these moments of self-care and reflection that you assimilate your insights, nurturing your mind, body, and spirit. Grant yourself permission to indulge in these practices, honoring the progress you've made and the path you're traversing toward a more enlightened and harmonious self.

As you journey through the transformative process of shadow work, it's essential to recognize the signs that indicate healing is taking place. These markers are subtle yet profound, signifying that you are moving in the right direction. Our Zenfulnote therapists have identified key indicators to help you acknowledge and celebrate your progress. Here are three signs that you're on the path to healing:

- **Integration of Your Shadows:** *Healing manifests as an increased awareness and acceptance of all parts of yourself, including those you might have previously overlooked or undervalued. This awareness can lead to earlier recognition of your triggers, fostering more harmonious self-talk and healthier interactions with others.*

- **Transformative Dream Patterns:** *As you heal, your dreams may evolve to mirror this positive change. They often start to exhibit themes of transformation and resolution, indicating that your unconscious conflicts are being worked through and reconciled.*

- **Increased Synchronicities:** *An intriguing sign of healing is the occurrence of meaningful coincidences in your life. These synchronicities, as Carl Jung termed them, suggest a deepening connection between your individual journey and the broader tapestry of the universe. They often appear as little affirmations or guides along your path of healing.*

If you recognize these signs in your own journey, take a moment to acknowledge your progress and the work you've put into your healing. These markers are a testament to your growth and the transformative power of your journey. Good work!

"UNLESS WE DO CONSCIOUS WORK ON IT,
THE SHADOW IS ALMOST ALWAYS PROJECTED;
THAT IS, IT IS NEATLY LAID ON SOMEONE
OR SOMETHING ELSE SO WE DO NOT HAVE
TO TAKE RESPONSIBILITY FOR IT."

—ROBERT A. JOHNSON,
author of *Owning Your Own Shadow*

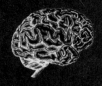

UNCONSCIOUS

- Habits + Patterns
- Emotions
- Protection
- Controls Bodily Functions
- Belief
- Desires
- Blaming, Denying, Lying
- Attachment to Things, Thoughts, Feelings

CONSCIOUS

- Logic

- Filter

- Analysis

- Movement

- Decision-Making

- Short-Term Memory

- Willpower

- Critical Thinking

2

Shadow Work Exercises

The process of training your mind to recognize your shadows can take time and effort. To help with this, it is recommended to set aside five to ten minutes each week to engage in a shadow work activity. This will give you the opportunity to intentionally reflect on your relationships, reactions, and inner thoughts.

It is important to remember that these exercises may cause discomfort or unease, but this is normal and a necessary part of the process. Use this chapter as a journal to record your discoveries and insights, and to monitor the evolution and development of your inner self over time.

You are encouraged to work through the shadow work activities at your own pace and in any order that suits you best.

Wound Mapping

EXERCISE:

To identify your inner child's wounds, examine the attributes listed on the following page. The four main types of inner child wounds are trust, guilt, neglect, and abandonment. It is possible that one or more of these may resonate with your personal experience.

WHY:

Being hurt or traumatized, particularly during childhood, can be deeply painful. This exercise aims to help you identify emotional wounds from your childhood that may still impact you today. These wounds often lead to negative behaviors and thought patterns that do not serve you well. By recognizing and understanding your inner child wound(s), you can cultivate a greater sense of self-compassion and lay the foundation for a successful shadow work journey.

TRUST WOUND

- Is afraid to be hurt
- Doesn't trust themselves
- Finds ways to not trust people
- Feels insecure and needs lots of external validation
- Doesn't feel safe
- Normally attracts people who don't make them feel safe

GUILT WOUND

- Feels "sorry" or "bad"
- Doesn't like to ask for things
- Uses guilt to manipulate
- Is afraid to set boundaries
- Normally attracts people who make them feel guilty

NEGLECT WOUND

- Struggles to let things go
- Has low self-worth
- Gets angry easily
- Struggles to say no
- Represses emotions
- Fears being vulnerable
- Normally attracts people who don't appreciate them or make them feel seen

ABANDONMENT WOUND

- Feels "left out"
- Fears being left
- Hates being alone
- Codependent
- Threatens to leave
- Normally attracts emotionally unavailable people

Fill in the Blank

EXERCISE:

Fill in the blank! Read through the paragraph and fill in the blanks without hesitation. If you can't come up with a word, try looking at your surroundings, find an object, and think of word associations for that object. Then, come back to the paragraph and try again.

WHY:

This series of "fill in the blank" shadow work exercises is a powerful practice that allows you to delve into your unconscious mind and explore the hidden aspects of yourself. By using selective words and word associations, you can gain a deeper understanding of your emotions, beliefs, and behaviors. This exercise provides an opportunity to shed light on the shadows that reside within you, and to gain greater self-awareness and insight into your inner workings.

$$\longrightarrow$$

**BEGIN "FILL IN THE BLANK" SERIES
ON THE NEXT PAGE**

PART 1

Fill in the Blank

I always feel like I'm the _____ one.

_____ is how I manage to escape.

_____ brings me peace.

I am so tired of _____ and

_____ but excited about

_____ and _____.

I want to try to _____ so that I can finally

_____.

For some reason, I always end up _____.

I deserve _____ and _____

_____.

Reflection Questions

Why am I sometimes seduced into a lack mentality?

What self-improvement techniques can I use to replace my negative thoughts with a more empowering belief about myself or the situation?

What kind of thinking do I need to adopt in order to step outside my limiting beliefs and focus on what excites me?

PART 2

Fill in the Blank

As a child I was told not to _____.

This made me very _____.

I feel like things would be different if _____

_____.

I wish I could tell my child self _____

_____.

I'm so grateful for _____, but wish my

guardians would have _____

_____.

Reflection Questions

What memories did I extract from this exercise?

How can I reframe these memories so that they don't continue to hurt and hinder me in the future?

How can I regularly serve myself with compassionate consolation as I would give to my child self?

PART 3

Fill in the Blank

_____ scares me the most. When I

become scared or anxious I tend to _____

_____. It sometimes sucks because _____

_____ and this

makes me feel _____.

My anxiety teaches me that _____ and

_____. I understand

that I am _____ but I love

myself unconditionally.

Reflection Questions

What is my current fear, and if it were to happen, what would be the best-case scenario?

If my fears and anxieties were teachers, what lessons would they teach me?

How can I build a more positive outlook on the unknown future?

PART 4

Fill in the Blank

_____ makes me tense.

I typically feel this tense sensation in my _____.

This makes me very _____. When this

happens, I start to _____. I think

this is because _____ and _____

_____. Next time I feel tense, I will

soothe myself by _____.

Reflection Questions

When does my anxiety take over my mind and body? Do I see a common recurring theme as to what triggers my anxiety?

What can I physically do to release my anxious energy and tension?

What thoughts help soothe my anxiety? How can I improve my self-talk to be less self-critical when these emotions arise?

PART 5

Fill in the Blank

As a child I was yelled at for _____.

My response was to _____ and

_____. After this, I've always been _____

_____. I care so much about

_____ and _____.

It triggers me now when _____.

I now hold a compassionate space for my full self and embrace this

part of me.

Reflection Questions

In what ways have I been reprimanded in my childhood and beyond?

How does this impact what I choose to do / not do in the present moment? In what ways am I holding back because of these experiences?

What activities can I partake in to fuel my inner child and allow myself to feel fully expressive?

PART 6

Fill in the Blank

As I grow older, I feel like the _____ part of me

becomes further and further away. I feel _____

toward this. Sometimes I put myself in a box by _____

_____. I understand that I

am ever changing and evolving each day. One way I can foster

my child self is by _____ and

_____. I will always recognize the

_____ part of me and show that version

of myself love and recognition.

Reflection Questions

What do I admire about my past self that I wish I could continue to foster more in the present day?

When/where do I find myself hiding parts of my personality in order to fit the mold?

What do I think would happen if I were to be my full self during these instances?

PART 7

Fill in the Blank

As a child, I used to cry when _____

_____. This made me emotional

because _____

_____.

The color of this sadness was _____ and it felt very

_____. I value _____

so much. If I could tell my child self anything in this situation, I

would say _____

_____

_____.

Reflection Questions

Is the reason for my sadness as a child connected to the reasons
I experience sadness as an adult?

How do I behave when I am experiencing sadness? Is this
behavioral reaction serving my highest self or not?

What can I do to release pain and sadness when it arises?
What are some things I love to do that lift my mood?

PART 8

Fill in the Blank

As a child, I wanted to be a _____

when I grew up. _____ and _____

_____ excited me so much!

Today, I get excited about_____ and

_____. As my passions and interests

evolve over time, I will hold space to nurture the things that bring

my child self joy. This could be by _____

or _____.

Reflection Questions

What excites me the most in life? How can I continue to foster this passion today?

What makes me unique and different?

What can I dream and imagine for myself now as an adult?

Release Stagnant Energy

EXERCISE:

Release trapped stagnant energy by choosing one of the activities on the next page. Become aware of how you feel both before and after your exercise is complete.

WHY:

Everything is energy in a world of both the physical and the metaphysical. When you feel "off," this means there is negative energy trapped in your body. Stagnant energy causes you to feel irritated and imbalanced. Many times, stagnant energy will manifest itself in the form of pain or tension in the body. Doing simple actions such as dancing, going on a walk, or meditating will help restore balance and unleash lingering stagnant energy stored within the body.

TOUCH THE
EARTH

STRETCH

DRAW OR
DOODLE

PUT ON A SONG
YOU LOVE
AND DANCE

WRITE A POEM

MAKE ART

DO A GRATITUDE
MEDITATION

BATHE IN THE
SUNLIGHT
FOR 10 MIN

GO FOR A WALK

TAKE A SHOWER.
ENVISION THE WATER
WASHING AWAY LINGERING
NEGATIVE ENERGY

Inner Child Affirmations

EXERCISE:

Find a mirror and, looking at your reflection, repeat the inner child affirmations on the next page out loud to yourself. Repeat the affirmations multiple times and notice how they begin to feel more natural and part of your inner truth.

WHY:

An affirmation is a positive phrase or statement that you can repeat to yourself on a daily or weekly cadence. By using affirmations, you can reprogram your mind to spotlight positive emotions and beliefs that may help you recover from negative self-narratives, suffering, and unhealthy habits. Once repeated enough times, an affirmation will embed into your inner consciousness—shifting old limiting thought patterns and unlocking new beliefs that help you reach your full potential. You can change the way you think, which will change the way you act, and help you become the person you want to be.

Inner Child Affirmations

- I release the feeling of guilt, hurt, and shame.

- I am protected.

- I accept every aspect of myself and my personality.

- I am loved.

- I am capable of every dream and worthy of every desire.

- I dream big.

- I am safe.

- I am beautiful and I accept myself for who I am.

- I honor the child within me.

- I show myself compassion.

- I am so much more than I thought I could be.

- My needs and feelings are valid.

- I deserve happiness.

- A feeling of peace comforts me.

- I am in control of my feelings.

- No one can inflict anything on me that I cannot handle.

- I love myself.

- I can protect myself.

- Setting firm boundaries comes easy for me.

- My energy is limitless.

Affirmations for the Trust, Guilt, Neglect, and Abandonment Wounds

EXERCISE:

Find a quiet, comfortable space where you won't be disturbed. Sit or stand in a relaxed posture, and close your eyes for a moment to center yourself. Open your eyes and, using a mirror, repeat the following affirmations out loud to yourself. Each set of affirmations corresponds to one of the four inner child wounds: Trust, Guilt, Neglect, and Abandonment. As you say each affirmation, focus on the sensation of the words, and allow yourself to fully experience their meaning. Additionally, this exercise includes affirmations aimed at fostering self-love and regulating your nervous system, further supporting your integration and grounding in the healing process.

WHY:

Affirmations are powerful tools for healing and transformation, especially when addressing deep-seated emotional wounds such as Trust, Guilt, Neglect, and Abandonment. These wounds often stem from early life experiences and can shape our beliefs and behaviors in adulthood.

Trust Affirmations

- I am learning to trust my intuition and inner wisdom.

- I embrace the reliability and strength within myself.

- Each day, I am building a foundation of trust in my relationships.

- I trust my journey and embrace uncertainty with courage.

- I am worthy of trust and give trust cautiously yet openly.

- I let go of past betrayals and open my heart to trust again.

- I trust in my strength to navigate through any situation.

- I honor my inner knowing and trust my path.

- I trust that I am guided by a higher wisdom and understanding.

- I am learning that trust starts within me and radiates outward.

- I trust in the unfolding of my life and welcome its lessons.

- Relaxing my mind is transforming my mind.

Guilt Affirmations

- I accept my past decisions and learn from them with compassion.

- I release myself from the weight of unnecessary guilt.

- I am more than my mistakes, and I grow stronger each day.

- I forgive myself and understand that feeling guilty is not my identity.

- I am learning to make choices that align with my values.

- I release shame and embrace the lessons it has taught me.

- My worth is not defined by my past.

- I am moving forward with a sense of peace and self-acceptance.

- I honor my feelings of guilt as guides toward better choices.

- I let go of guilt and make space for joy and self-compassion.

- I choose to forgive myself.

- I am not defined by the guilt I feel but by the resilience I show.

Neglect Affirmations

- I am worthy of attention and care.

- I choose to surround myself with people who value and respect me.

- I am learning to recognize and meet my own needs.

- I am healing from neglect and growing into my best self.

- I am deserving of a life filled with love, care, and attention.

- I recognize my worth and advocate for my own needs.

- I deserve to be seen, heard, and cared for.

- I am confident in expressing my needs and seeking fulfillment.

- I am healing from neglect by nurturing my body, mind, and soul.

- I am creating a life that reflects my values and worth.

- I am breaking the cycle of neglect and choosing a path of self-empowerment.

- I am worthy of a nurturing and attentive environment.

Abandonment Affirmations

- I am whole within myself and do not need validation from others.

- I release the fear of abandonment and embrace my own company.

- I am deserving of stable, lasting relationships.

- It is extremely healthy to have my own thoughts, ideas, feelings, and beliefs.

- I am surrounded by love and support, even when I am alone.

- I am creating a life where I feel secure, valued, and connected.

- My worth is not diminished by the actions or absence of others.

- I am resilient and capable of overcoming fears of abandonment.

- I am deserving of lasting and nurturing connections.

- I find comfort and strength within myself, always.

- I am not alone; I am part of a universe that supports and nurtures me.

- I celebrate the strength I've found in facing and healing abandonment.

Affirmations of Self-Love

- I am worthy of love and respect from myself and others.

- I embrace my uniqueness and celebrate my individuality.

- I am enough just as I am.

- I treat myself with kindness, patience, and understanding.

- I am deserving of happiness and fulfillment.

- I respect my boundaries and honor my needs.

- I am a valuable and important person.

- My self-worth is independent of others' opinions or actions.

- I am proud of who I am and who I am becoming.

- I love myself deeply and unconditionally.

- I am committed to my personal growth and well-being.

- I choose to see the beauty and strength within me.

Affirmations for Nervous System Regulation

- I am safe and at peace in this moment.

- I allow my body to relax and release tension.

- I breathe in calmness and breathe out stress.

- My mind is calm, and my body is relaxed.

- I am in control of my responses to stress.

- With each breath, I feel more serene and centered.

- I allow myself to experience and release my emotions safely.

- I absorb the nature of this world.

- I am gentle with myself during times of anxiety or stress.

- I trust in my ability to navigate through challenging emotions.

- I give myself permission to slow down and rest.

- My body knows how to restore balance and harmony.

THE PROCESS OF INTEGRATING SHADOWS IS AKIN TO ALCHEMY—AN INNER TRANSMUTATION WHERE WE TURN OUR WOUNDS INTO WISDOM, OUR FEARS INTO COURAGE, AND OUR LIMITATIONS INTO BOUNDLESS POTENTIAL.

A Letter to Your Past Self

EXERCISE:

Find some time to take a step back from your normal routine and do a deep reflection. Think back to a difficulty you faced in the past, and write a letter addressed to that version of yourself. Write your letter with love and empathy. Share the advice you needed to hear. The content of your letter should be unique to your experience. Start with one sentence and see where your heart flows.

WHY:

Writing a letter to your past self is therapeutic and will help you gain closure, clarity, and inner peace. Your inner child is still inside of you, waiting to be heard and nurtured. You may even find that this letter will resonate with you in the future.

To My Past Self ...

Mirror Gazing

EXERCISE:

Find a mirror that you can sit down in front of. Take a seat and get close up to the mirror so that you can gaze into your eyes. Spend five to ten minutes looking directly into your eyes, and try your best not to look away. If you feel comfortable, talk to your reflection and have a conversation with your shadow. When you are done, tell yourself that you are safe and loved.

WHY:

Mirror gazing is an intimate way to face your deepest fears and insecurities. During mirror gazing, you may begin to see aspects of yourself that repulse you. You may come across thoughts, doubts, and fears that keep you from experiencing peace. You may even see physical parts of yourself shifting, magnifying, or aging. Do not be alarmed or repulsed if this happens. Show yourself compassion and love. This exercise will allow you to mentally wrestle with yourself and surrender to your insecurities.

Find a mirror and sit in front of it closely. Spend five to ten minutes gazing at yourself. Try your best not to look away. Talk to your reflection as if it were your shadow self.

Afterward, answer the reflective questions below:

What recurring thoughts did I have? _____

_____

What emotions arose? _____

_____

How do I feel now? _____

_____

What conversations did I have? What breakthroughs did I discover?

_____

_____

_____

_____

_____

_____

Fill in the Box

EXERCISE:

Read the prompts on the next page and respond by filling each box provided with your authentic answer.

WHY:

You are shaped by your experiences. Reflective writing prompts will guide you toward understanding who you are and why. This will help you recognize positive and negative patterns and habits impacting your view on life.

Do I feel guilty if I put my needs first?

_____

How important is my own happiness?

_____

In what ways do I show love to myself?

_____

I think I still need to work on . . .

_____

Visualization Meditation

MEET YOUR SHADOW

EXERCISE:

This exercise is a visualization meditation that you will access by scanning the QR code on the next page. Make sure that you are in a room or a setting without distractions. You may do the meditation with or without headphones. To begin the visualization meditation, find a comfortable position and take a few deep breaths.

WHY:

Visualization meditation is a powerful technique used to connect with your inner self. When you merge with your shadow self, it can help you to gain insight into the parts of yourself that you have been blocking off or trying to ignore.

LISTEN
TO THE VISUALIZATION
MEDITATION

HERE.

EXERCISE:

This exercise is a visualization meditation that you will access by scanning the QR code on the next page. Make sure that you are in a room or a setting without distractions. You may do the meditation with or without headphones. To begin the visualization meditation, find a comfortable position and take a few deep breaths.

WHY:

Visualization meditation is a powerful technique used to connect with your inner self. When you merge with your shadow self, it can help you to gain insight into the parts of yourself that you have been blocking off or trying to ignore.

LISTEN
TO THE VISUALIZATION
MEDITATION

HERE.

Breath Work

EASE YOUR ANXIETY

EXERCISE:

A basic breath work activity to help calm the nervous system involves sitting in a comfortable position, closing your eyes, and taking deep, slow breaths. You will be guided into a breath work exercise by scanning the code on the next page.

WHY:

Breath work is a powerful tool that can be used to help calm the nervous system and bring the body into a state of greater relaxation. It involves conscious control of breathing and the use of specific breathing techniques. By focusing on certain breathing patterns, we can help to reduce the body's stress response, decrease the activity of the sympathetic nervous system, and increase the activity of the parasympathetic nervous system. This can help to reduce our stress levels, increase our ability to relax, and improve our overall well-being.

LISTEN
TO THE BREATH WORK
MEDITATION

HERE.

EXERCISE:

A basic breath work activity to help calm the nervous system involves sitting in a comfortable position, closing your eyes, and taking deep, slow breaths. You will be guided into a breath work exercise by scanning the QR code on the next page.

WHY:

Breath work is a powerful tool that can be used to help calm the nervous system and bring the body into a state of greater relaxation. It involves conscious control of breathing and the use of specific breathing techniques. By focusing on certain breathing patterns, we can help to reduce the body's stress response, decrease the activity of the sympathetic nervous system, and increase the activity of the parasympathetic nervous system. This can help to reduce our stress levels, increase our ability to relax, and improve our overall well-being.

LISTEN
TO THE BREATH WORK
MEDITATION

HERE.

3

Integrate Your
Shadow Exercises

EFT Tapping

Meditation: Integrate Your Shadow

Gratitude List

Inner Child Creative Embodiment

Cultivating Gratitude

Exploring Joy

Cognitive Reframing

Ancestral Healing

This part of The Shadow Work Journal *represents a significant transition from discovering the hidden facets of your personality to integrating these aspects into a cohesive self. These exercises were meticulously designed with the help of Zenfulnote therapists to guide you in blending the often overlooked parts of your psyche—your shadow aspects— with your conscious self, fostering a more balanced and authentic existence.*

These activities will encourage you to confront and engage with the parts of yourself that have remained in the dark, bringing them into the light of acceptance and understanding. This process is crucial for achieving a sense of wholeness and authenticity, as it allows you to fully acknowledge and integrate all aspects of your being.

Each exercise is an invitation to explore how your shadow elements, once acknowledged, can be transformed into positive forces in your life. Rather than viewing these aspects as hindrances, you'll learn to see them as valuable components of your identity that, when harnessed correctly, can bolster your strengths and resilience. These exercises are about redefining your relationship with your shadow self, and recognizing its potential to contribute positively to your life.

EFT Tapping

EXERCISE:

EFT in five simple steps:

1. **State the problem**
2. **Identify the level of pain**
3. **Create your setup statement**
4. **Tap the points**
5. **Re-check the level of pain**

Tips: Be specific, focus on the negative, and try it on everything; come back to EFT tapping anytime you are worried, upset, anxious, angry, or annoyed.

Example setup statements: "I deeply love and completely accept myself," "I forgive myself as best as I can," "I want to get to a calm, peaceful place."

WHY:

EFT tapping can be used to work through difficult emotions and gain insight into the root cause of them. It can also be used to do shadow work. By tapping on the acupressure points and allowing yourself to become aware of the emotions associated with these parts of yourself, you can begin to accept, integrate, and heal them. EFT tapping can help you to gain clarity and insight into the underlying causes of your repressed feelings.

FOLLOW YOUR EFT SESSION BELOW

1. Take a few deep breaths and begin tapping on the specific points of the body associated with EFT: the eyebrow points, the side of the eye, under the eye, under the nose, the chin, the collarbone, and under the arm.

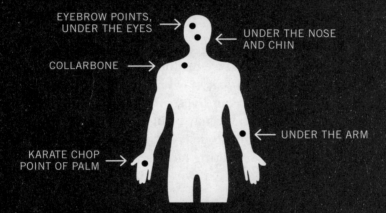

EYEBROW POINTS, UNDER THE EYES →

→ UNDER THE NOSE AND CHIN

COLLARBONE →

← UNDER THE ARM

KARATE CHOP POINT OF PALM →

2. As you tap, repeat the affirmation statement that resonates with the issue that you are exploring. For example, if you are exploring a fear of failure, you could say, "Even though I'm scared of failing, I accept and love myself."

3. During the tapping process, focus on the issue at hand and allow yourself to feel any emotions that come up. Spend the next two to three minutes tapping and repeating your mantra.

4. Once you feel like you have released some of the energy and emotion associated with the issue, take a few deep breaths and reflect on what you have learned. What insight have you gained? How can you use this insight to move forward in a positive and constructive way?

Gratitude List

EXERCISE:

Take five minutes to create a gratitude list. Think of all the things that bring you health, peace, and love. List both big and small things in life, from your home appliances to your relationships with others. If it feels right, acknowledge the things that brought you pain in the past but have taught you patience and healing. When your list is complete, take a moment to say "thank you" to each one for existing and making you who you are.

WHY:

Psychologist Dr. Rick Hanson suggests that the brain takes the shape of the state of mind we rest upon. If we rest upon doubt, sadness, and irritability, it may bring more anger, anxiety, and depression into our lives. And if we rest upon joy, contentment, and love, we may bring more abundance and peace into our lives. Gratitude is a wonderful way of improving your life and creating more abundance by appreciating what you currently have.

Gratitude List

♥ _____

♥ _____

♥ _____

♥ _____

♥ _____

♥ _____

♥ _____

♥ _____

♥ _____

♥ _____

♥ _____

♥ _____

Inner Child Creative Embodiment

EXERCISE:

In this activity, you'll explore the world of your inner child, rekindling the sense of playfulness and wonder that resides within. Reconnecting with your inner child can be a deeply healing and joyful experience. Looking at a photograph of your child self can be a helpful addition to this practice.

WHY:

This practice enhances self-awareness, reconnecting you with your true passions and desires from childhood. It serves as a stress reliever, providing a break from adult responsibilities and ushering in relaxation and joy.
The exercise taps into your innate creativity, fostering imaginative thinking and problem-solving. It strengthens the mind-body connection, enhancing overall well-being. By engaging with your inner child, you practice self-compassion and acceptance, which are key to developing a positive self-image. This activity rekindles the joy and playfulness often lost in adulthood, bringing lightness to your life.

STEP 1: Create a Safe Space

Find a comfortable, quiet space where you won't
be disturbed. You may want to sit or lie down.
Time: 1 minute

STEP 2: Remember Childhood Play

Close your eyes and reflect on your inner child. How old
are you? What do you look like? What do you get excited
about? What type of play, games, or activities do you
love? What brought you pure joy and laughter when you
were that age? Take time to let those playful memories
resurface. **Time: 5 minutes**

STEP 3: Play Imaginatively

Now imagine watching your child self engage in a favorite
childhood activity. Visualize the sensory experience: What
sights, sounds, smells, tastes, touches, and feelings
do you associate with this time? Allow yourself to fully
immerse in this experience. **Time: 5 minutes**

STEP 4: Express Yourself

Release your inner child's energy by engaging in creative
expression. You can draw, paint, dance, sing, write,
build, or anything else that comes to mind. Let your
creativity and connection to your child self flow freely.
Time: 10–30 minutes

Cultivating Gratitude

EXERCISE:

A gratitude practice is a ritual that will help you improve your mood, decrease stress hormones, and shift your mindset into a positive one. With just five minutes in the morning and five minutes before bed, you can shift your life into a reality with more meaningful connections and experiences. Dive into the next page, and let's begin to practice gratitude.

WHY:

The practice of daily gratitude has profound benefits for both mental and emotional well-being. It's a deliberate shift in focus from deficits to abundance, inherently improving mood and reducing stress. This simple yet powerful act fosters deeper connections with others, enhancing relationships through the recognition and appreciation of their positive aspects. Engaging in gratitude brings about mindfulness, encouraging presence in the moment, and appreciation of life's small joys. It builds emotional resilience, equipping you to face challenges with a more positive perspective. Studies also suggest that gratitude can improve physical health, leading to better sleep and potentially lower blood pressure. Cultivating gratitude transforms not just how you see the world but how you experience it.

STEP 1: Settling into the Morning

After you wake up, prepare your morning routine. It could include making tea or coffee, brushing your teeth, or whatever you typically do to kick off your day. Then, gather your journal, writing materials, and any other morning routine items that make you feel grounded and prepared. Settle into your morning space, where you will have at least five minutes of undisturbed time.

Time: 5 minutes

STEP 2: Intention Setting

After you have settled in, take a deep breath in, close your eyes, and release the breath fully. Allow your breath to be natural, inhaling and exhaling through the nose. Begin to focus on the intention of your day, whether it is a word, feeling, or visualization. **Time: 1 minute**

STEP 3: Morning Gratitude Practice

Once you have connected to your daily intention, open your eyes. Take out your journal and prepare to reflect on the following morning prompts: "What are three things that can put a smile on someone else's face today?" and "What are three ways for you to have a smile on your face today?" Try to spend about sixty to ninety seconds on each prompt. **Time: 3 minutes**

STEP 4: Evening Gratitude Practice

Once you have reflected on your daily intention, open your eyes. Take out your journal and prepare to reflect on the following evening prompts: "How did you put a smile on someone else's face today?" and "What made you smile today?" Try to spend about sixty to ninety seconds on each prompt. **Time: 3 minutes**

ONLY BY FACING THESE HIDDEN ASPECTS
CAN WE HOPE TO LIVE FULLY, BOUND
NEITHER BY FEAR NOR ILLUSION,
BUT PROPELLED BY A PROFOUND
UNDERSTANDING OF OUR COMPLEX
NATURE.

"Everything that irritates us about others can
lead to an understanding of ourselves."
—CARL JUNG

Exploring Joy

EXERCISE:

In this activity, we will explore a reimagined version of our lives through some structured self-reflection. We will explore what we would attempt if failure weren't an option; how we would want to be remembered if today were our last day on earth; who we would bring unlimited joy to, and how we would describe happiness. By taking these steps, we can tap into our deepest desires and aspirations.

WHY:

This exercise helps in shedding the usual constraints of fear and doubt, enabling you to explore what you would truly desire if failure weren't a factor. It encourages you to think expansively about your ambitions, passions, and dreams. By contemplating how you would like to be remembered, the exercise guides you to reflect on your values and the legacy you wish to leave, which can reshape your current priorities and actions. Considering whom you would bring unlimited joy to not only focuses on your capacity to positively impact others but also deepens your understanding of meaningful relationships in your life. Describing happiness as a color allows for a creative and personal interpretation of joy, helping to solidify your unique concept of happiness. This is a powerful tool for reimagining your life's possibilities, understanding your core values, and manifesting a life that aligns with your deepest sense of joy and purpose.

STEP 1: **If failure weren't an option, what would I attempt?**

In this step, you will envision what you would dare to pursue if you knew you couldn't fail. Imagine there are no limitations. Take a few moments to reflect on your dreams, passions, and ambitions. Imagine the possibilities and allow yourself to dream big.
Time: 3 minutes

STEP 2: **If today were my last day on earth, how would I be remembered?**

Contemplate your legacy and the impact you want to leave behind. Reflect on how you would like to be remembered by your loved ones, your community, and the world. Consider the values, contributions, and qualities you would like to be remembered for.
Time: 3 minutes

STEP 3: **If I could give unlimited joy to one person in my life, who would it be?**

In this step, you will focus on the power of bringing happiness to others. Think about someone special in your life and imagine the joy you could bring them if there were no limitations. Reflect on the ways you could make a positive difference in their life and the happiness it would bring to both of you. **Time: 3 minutes**

STEP 4: **If happiness were a color, how would you describe it?**

Imagine happiness as a color and try to describe it in your own words. Reflect on the emotions, sensations, and experiences that come to mind when you think of happiness. **Time: 3 minutes**

Cognitive Reframing

EXERCISE:

The Socratic method, renowned for its open-ended questioning approach, is an effective tool for self-reflection and cognitive reframing. This exercise combines this method with your intuition to challenge and transform negative thought patterns into positive, growth-oriented ones. By intuitively asking yourself targeted questions, you can uncover subconscious answers and reshape your thinking.

WHY:

The intuitive Socratic questioning technique for Cognitive Reframing is a transformative practice with multiple benefits. It effectively challenges and disrupts negative thought patterns, facilitating a shift toward more rational and positive thinking. This exercise promotes a deeper level of self-awareness, as it encourages you to explore and understand the roots of your thoughts, including underlying beliefs and emotional triggers. As you replace negative thoughts with positive affirmations, you cultivate a positive mindset, which is essential for overall mental well-being. This method enhances mental flexibility and resilience, enabling you to adapt more easily to life's challenges.

STEP 1: Identify the Thought Pattern

This activity begins the moment you have a negative/ heavy thought pattern that activates anxiety and/or depression in the body, starts arguments with others, or perhaps induces procrastination. For example, "I am depressed being home alone because no one wants to hang out with me." Once you notice this thought pattern, take a moment to retreat to your own space while you recollect and decompress.
Time: 1 minute

STEP 2: Settle into Awareness

After you have settled into your space, take a deep breath in, close your eyes, and release the breath fully. Allow your breath to be natural, inhaling and exhaling through the nose. Begin to focus on the experience that initiated the thought pattern. **Time: 1 minute**

STEP 3: Ask Intuitive Questions

You will begin to internally ask yourself intuitive questions, to dive deeper into the initial thought pattern. Begin with one question at a time, based on the experience in question, and reflect on the intuitive prompt. Here are a few starting examples: "Is this thought realistic?"; "Am I basing this thought in reality or fantasy?"; "Can I be misinterpreting this experience?"; "Am I having this thought out of habit or are there facts that support it?" Continue this process until you feel ready to reframe the initial thought.
Time: 3 minutes

STEP 4: Reframe Thought Pattern

Once you have decompressed the initial thought, replace it with a positive thought pattern. For example: if the initial thought was "I am depressed being home alone because no one wants to hang out with me," you will replace it with "I am spending some alone time tonight, so I can do whatever I want!" **Time: 3 minutes**

STEP 5: Identify, Question, Reframe, Repeat

Continue Steps 1–4 with each triggered thought pattern. You may only have one thought pattern a day, or multiple thought patterns. As you begin this mind-reframing practice, it is normal to have multiple thought patterns at the start. As you continue to reframe, you will find that the number of thought patterns that trigger you will lessen and lessen. Be gentle with yourself and take your time, healing doesn't happen overnight.

Time: 9 minutes

What insights did you have about this exercise?

_____

_____

_____

_____

_____

_____

Ancestral Healing

EXERCISE:

In the ancestral healing meditation, you begin by finding a quiet space to relax and focus on deep breathing, preparing your body and mind for the session. You then visualize your ancestors, allowing them to present to you a generational wound that needs healing. This wound is observed and experienced through your senses, helping you understand its nature and emotional impact. Any emotional response to the wound, such as sadness or anger, is released through expressive means like crying or deep breathing. Initiating the ancestral healing meditation draws upon the Mini-Ho'oponopono—a revered Hawaiian tradition of reconciliation and forgiveness. Visualizing your ancestors, you identify a generational wound to explore through your senses, understanding its emotional impact. Emotional releases, such as crying or deep breathing, are encouraged as part of the healing, which culminates in repeating a powerful affirmation to heal the wound. This practice, which can be revisited for various wounds, offers a new opportunity for profound healing and insight each time.

WHY:

Ancestral healing is a profound practice that addresses not only individual healing but also the healing of generational lines. It's based on the understanding that some emotional, psychological, and even physical wounds can be passed down from one generation to another. By identifying these inherited wounds, we can begin to heal patterns that may have been affecting our family for generations. This form of healing is not only about understanding the past but also about transforming the future. It allows us to release inherited trauma, preventing it from being passed down to subsequent generations.

> "I am not what happened to me. I am what I choose to become."
> —CARL JUNG

STEP 1: Preparing the Body

Find a seat in a quiet place where you feel safe and will be uninterrupted. Sit with your spine tall and your shoulders relaxed. Close your eyes and breathe gently in and out through your nose. Take three deep-ocean breaths, allowing the belly to expand fully on the inhale and releasing the breath fully on the exhale.
Time: 3 minutes

STEP 2: Calling in Your Ancestors

Begin to visualize your ancestors appearing before you. Allow them to show themselves one at a time. Not just ancestors from past centuries, but current ancestors as well (parents, grandparents, great-grandparents, etc.). If you are not a practiced visualizer, you can feel this experience in your body instead. **Time: 3 minutes**

STEP 3: Presenting the Wound

When you feel ready, allow the ancestor to present to you a generational wound that is ready to be brought to the healing surface. There is no need to overthink it; use the first wound the ancestor presents. If you feel or visualize several wounds, process one at a time and restart at this step for each new wound. **Time: 3 minutes**

STEP 4: Wound Reflection

Once you have surfaced the wound, experience it with your senses. Does the wound make you feel angry, sad, depressed, excited, etc.? Is it cold or warm? Is the wound old or new? Does the wound have a shape or color or maybe an odor? Gather a clear visualization or feeling of the wound. **Time: 3 minutes**

STEP 5: **Wound Release**

If you feel emotionally charged from the wound, allow yourself to cry, yell, or continue deep breathing to release the emotions. Whatever emotion you may feel arises with the wound, allow it to move through your body without attaching to it and taking it on personally. You are observing inner wounds to bring them to light, heal them, and release them.

Time: 3 minutes

STEP 6: **Wound Renewal (Mini-Ho'oponopono)**

Once you have a clear visualization or feeling of the wound, you will repeat the following phrases aloud nine times: "I am sorry; please forgive me; thank you; I love you." You can ask your ancestors to assist you in repeating this affirmation aloud. Visualize or feel the wound as you are saying this affirmation. You are having a confirmation with the wound, as if it were a living thing with which you can communicate.

Time: 3 minutes

STEP 7: **Wound Heal, Repeat**

If you have other wounds you want to work on, go back to Step 3 and repeat Steps 3–6. You can do several in one session, or you can do multiple sessions for one wound. Be easy on yourself and don't rush your healing. Allow yourself time to process your meditations and healing sessions. A journal is a great friend for this exercise, especially if you plan to do it more than once.

Time: 3 minutes

4

Journal
Prompts

Inner Child	Inner Teen
Self	Anxiety
Fears	Jealousy
Anger	Strengths
Sadness	Dream Life

Journaling is a powerful tool to unravel your emotions and beliefs. Writing about your experiences helps you become more aware, intuitive, and present. For as little as ten minutes per day, journaling can change the way you behave and think.

Use these shadow work journaling prompts to lean into your unconscious mind and build an understanding of your shadow. Please note that these journaling prompts get deep and dark, but do not let that hold you back.

Parental Influence

What parts of your parents or guardians do you notice reflected in yourself?

_____

_____

_____

_____

_____

_____

_____

_____

_____

_____

_____

_____

_____

_____

What traits, both good and bad, have you inherited from them?

_____

_____

_____

_____

_____

_____

How can you break the negative behavioral chains that run through your family?

_____

_____

_____

_____

_____

_____

_____

Traits

Which traits do you wish to improve about yourself?

_____

_____

_____

_____

_____

_____

_____

_____

_____

_____

_____

_____

_____

When do these traits most commonly present themselves?

_____

_____

_____

_____

_____

How can you show these parts of yourself compassion and love?

_____

_____

_____

_____

_____

_____

Childhood

In your childhood, what did you not receive?

How has this impacted you?

_____

_____

_____

_____

_____

What do you think would be different if you had received this?

_____

_____

_____

_____

_____

_____

Childhood Trauma

What experiences did you have as a child that impacted
you in a negative way?

_____

_____

_____

_____

_____

_____

_____

_____

_____

_____

_____

_____

_____

What impact did these experiences have on you as a child?

_____

_____

_____

_____

_____

How are these experiences still impacting you today
(how you think, feel, and relate to others)?

_____

_____

_____

_____

_____

_____

Putting Yourself Last

Where in your life are you putting yourself last?

_____

_____

_____

_____

_____

_____

_____

_____

_____

_____

_____

_____

_____

How does putting yourself last impact your overall well-being, happiness, and fulfillment?

_____

_____

_____

_____

_____

Why did you put aside your own well-being and needs?

_____

_____

_____

_____

_____

@zenfulnote   Zenfulnote   DATE: /   /   /

How do you think others see you?

_____

_____

_____

_____

_____

_____

_____

_____

_____

_____

How would you like to be seen and why?
What do you appreciate most about yourself?

_____

_____

_____

_____

_____

What do you believe is the most authentic version of yourself?
How often are you able to be your most authentic self?

_____

_____

_____

_____

_____

_____

_____

Authentic Self

Your authentic self is what hides behind layers of learned masks.
Is there anything you wish more people knew about you?

_____

_____

_____

_____

_____

_____

_____

_____

_____

_____

_____

_____

Why don't more people know about your authentic self already?

_____

_____

_____

_____

_____

In what ways would your relationships look different if people knew about your authentic self?

_____

_____

_____

_____

_____

_____

Less

Reflect on everything you have, both physical and nonphysical.

_____

_____

_____

_____

_____

_____

_____

_____

_____

_____

_____

_____

Sometimes things can energetically weigh down our quality of living. What is weighing you down?

_____

_____

_____

_____

_____

What could you have less of in your life to feel more freedom and peace?

_____

_____

_____

_____

_____

_____

Secrets

What is your biggest secret?

_____

_____

_____

_____

_____

_____

_____

_____

_____

_____

_____

_____

_____

_____

Why is this a secret? Have you ever shared it with anyone?

_____

_____

_____

_____

_____

_____

How would you feel if others knew about your secret?

_____

_____

_____

_____

_____

_____

_____

Fear

Imagine yourself unafraid. You have no doubts, no worries, no fears of the unknown. The things you used to worry about do not exist. Write about what you would do if you had no fear.

_____

_____

_____

_____

_____

_____

_____

_____

_____

_____

_____

_____

In what ways would your life look different?

_____

_____

_____

_____

_____

How would it feel to let go of the fear you hold?

_____

_____

_____

_____

_____

_____

_____

Identify Your Fear

What is fear to you?

_____

_____

_____

_____

_____

_____

_____

_____

_____

_____

_____

_____

_____

_____

What makes you afraid?

_____

_____

_____

_____

_____

Instead of writing "I am afraid of . . . ," phrase it as
"I experience fear when . . ." This will allow you to break
the habit of identifying fear as part of yourself.

_____

_____

_____

_____

_____

Nightmares

Describe the most vivid nightmare you remember.

_____

_____

_____

_____

_____

_____

_____

_____

_____

_____

_____

_____

_____

_____

_____

_____

_____

How did it make you feel? Are there any patterns, symbols, or common themes?

_____

_____

_____

_____

_____

Explore the emotions that the nightmare evoked.

_____

_____

_____

_____

_____

_____

Facing Your Fear

What is your biggest fear in life?

_____

_____

_____

_____

_____

_____

_____

_____

_____

_____

_____

_____

How does this fear affect your daily life and decision-making?

_____

_____

_____

_____

_____

Have you tried to confront or overcome the fear in the past?
If so, what strategies did you use? If not, what might be holding
you back?

_____

_____

_____

_____

_____

@zenfulnote   Zenfulnote   DATE: /   /   /

Avoidance

What do you try your best to avoid in life?

_____

_____

_____

_____

_____

_____

_____

_____

_____

_____

_____

_____

_____

Why do you try to avoid these things?

_____

_____

_____

_____

_____

_____

Are there certain emotions attached to these things that you
don't want to experience?

_____

_____

_____

_____

_____

_____

_____

_____

Personal Change

What are ten ways you have changed in the past ten years?

_____

_____

_____

_____

_____

_____

_____

_____

_____

_____

_____

_____

_____

_____

How did these changes impact you?

_____

_____

_____

_____

_____

_____

Are these changes mainly positive or negative?

_____

_____

_____

_____

_____

_____

_____

Changes

Change is a natural part of life, yet our response to it can be a choice. Do you embrace change, or do you avoid it?

_____

_____

_____

_____

_____

_____

_____

_____

_____

_____

_____

_____

_____

_____

How well do you handle change?

_____

_____

_____

_____

_____

_____

Why do you think this is?

_____

_____

_____

_____

_____

_____

_____

Energy Drainers

Think back to the last time you were drained.

_____

_____

_____

_____

_____

_____

_____

_____

_____

_____

_____

_____

What were you doing? Who were you with?

_____

_____

_____

_____

_____

_____

What did you need at that moment?

_____

_____

_____

_____

_____

_____

_____

Critical Thoughts

What moments or situations cause you to be the hardest
on yourself?

_____

_____

_____

_____

_____

_____

_____

_____

_____

_____

_____

_____

What factors lead you to respond to yourself in this way?

_____

_____

_____

_____

_____

_____

How do you feel when you become hypercritical of yourself?
In what ways could you be more compassionate and
understanding toward yourself?

_____

_____

_____

_____

_____

Tolerance

What are you tolerating that you do not want to be tolerating?

_____

_____

_____

_____

_____

_____

_____

_____

_____

_____

_____

_____

Think of any self-sabotaging behaviors and question why you continue to repeat those negative actions and/or thoughts.

_____

_____

_____

_____

_____

_____

How would it feel to let go of self-sabotage?

_____

_____

_____

_____

_____

_____

Anger Triggers

What makes you angry?

_____

_____

_____

_____

_____

_____

_____

_____

_____

_____

_____

_____

_____

What factors lead you to feel this way?

_____

_____

_____

_____

_____

How do you cope with your anger, and how does this impact your life?

_____

_____

_____

_____

_____

_____

Anger

What are you most angry about right now?

_____

_____

_____

_____

_____

_____

_____

_____

_____

_____

_____

_____

_____

_____

Why is this making you angry?

_____

_____

_____

_____

_____

Where in your body do you feel this anger? How does the anger
feel in your body?

_____

_____

_____

_____

_____

_____

Self-Talk

How do you speak to yourself when you're angry with yourself?

_____

_____

_____

_____

_____

_____

_____

_____

_____

_____

_____

_____

_____

Does it differ from how you speak to yourself when you're angry with other people?

_____

_____

_____

_____

_____

How does this self-talk impact you?

_____

_____

_____

_____

_____

_____

The Color of Anger

What color is your anger?

_____

_____

_____

_____

_____

_____

_____

_____

_____

_____

_____

_____

Why is it this color?

_____

_____

_____

_____

_____

How does it make you feel?

_____

_____

_____

_____

_____

_____

Anger Relievers

What causes your anger to melt away?

_____

_____

_____

_____

_____

_____

_____

_____

_____

_____

_____

_____

_____

_____

How easy is it to dissipate your anger?

_____

_____

_____

_____

_____

How can you implement this anger reliever in your day-to-day life?

_____

_____

_____

_____

_____

_____

Sadness

What would your sadness look like if it were a painting or a drawing? (You don't actually have to sketch it out, but instead, use words to visualize it.)

_____

_____

_____

_____

_____

_____

_____

_____

_____

_____

_____

_____

What colors and shapes would your sadness have?

_____

_____

_____

_____

_____

How big would your sadness be, and how much space would it take up?

_____

_____

_____

_____

_____

_____

Sadness Self-Talk

How do you talk to yourself when you're feeling sad?

_____

_____

_____

_____

_____

_____

_____

_____

_____

_____

_____

_____

_____

_____

What tone of voice do you use when talking to yourself?

_____

_____

_____

_____

_____

Are you showing yourself compassion, or are you frustrated or annoyed?

_____

_____

_____

_____

_____

Mixed Emotions

Are you experiencing any other emotions outside of
your sadness?

_____

_____

_____

_____

_____

_____

_____

_____

_____

_____

_____

_____

_____

How do these feelings sit alongside the sadness?

_____

_____

_____

_____

_____

Can you find where you're holding these feelings in your body?

_____

_____

_____

_____

_____

_____

Negative Thoughts

What negative thoughts are you currently experiencing?

_____

_____

_____

_____

_____

_____

_____

_____

_____

_____

_____

_____

_____

_____

_____

_____

What are five positive thoughts for each of those negative thoughts?

_____

_____

_____

_____

_____

How does negative thinking impact you?

_____

_____

_____

_____

_____

_____

Holding On

What are you holding on to that still hurts you deeply?

_____

_____

_____

_____

_____

_____

_____

_____

_____

_____

_____

_____

_____

What feelings or emotions are associated with what you're holding on to?

_____

_____

_____

_____

_____

How would it feel if you let it go?

_____

_____

_____

_____

_____

_____

Love Letter

Write a love letter to yourself, expressing all the things you need to hear. Have compassion for yourself and explore all the parts of yourself that are worthy of celebrating.

_____

_____

_____

_____

_____

_____

_____

_____

_____

_____

_____

_____

_____

_____

Teenage Hero

Who was your teenage hero?

What qualities did they display that you were drawn to?

_____

_____

_____

_____

_____

Do you still feel the same admiration for that hero today?

_____

_____

_____

_____

_____

_____

Past Friendships

Who were your closest friends growing up?

_____

_____

_____

_____

_____

_____

_____

_____

_____

_____

_____

_____

_____

What feelings come to the surface when you reflect on these relationships?

_____

_____

_____

_____

_____

Are these friends still in your life today? If so, have the friendships changed? If your friends are not still in your life, why did the friendships end?

_____

_____

_____

_____

_____

Teachers

Who were your favorite teachers at school?

How did these teachers have an impact on you?

_____

_____

_____

_____

_____

_____

If you were to see your favorite teachers again, what would you say to them?

_____

_____

_____

_____

_____

_____

_____

Inner Teen

What do you wish someone would have told you as a teenager?

_____

_____

_____

_____

_____

_____

_____

_____

_____

_____

_____

_____

_____

_____

How has not hearing those words impacted you?

_____

_____

_____

_____

_____

If you had heard those words as a teenager, how do you think your life would be different today?

_____

_____

_____

_____

_____

_____

Teenage Events

What major events happened to you as a teenager?

_____

_____

_____

_____

_____

_____

_____

_____

_____

_____

_____

_____

_____

_____

How did these events impact you?

_____

_____

_____

_____

_____

Do these events still have an impact on your life today?
If so, how do they continue to define who you are?

_____

_____

_____

_____

_____

_____

_____

Admiring Your Teen Self

What do you admire about your teenage self?

_____

_____

_____

_____

_____

_____

_____

_____

_____

_____

_____

_____

What traits did you have as a teenager that you've carried through to the present day?

_____

_____

_____

_____

_____

_____

Are there any traits that you would like to reclaim?

_____

_____

_____

_____

_____

_____

_____

Teenage Lessons

What are the biggest lessons you learned in your teenage years?

_____

_____

_____

_____

_____

_____

_____

_____

_____

_____

_____

_____

_____

How did those lessons motivate you as a teenager?

_____

_____

_____

_____

_____

_____

How have those lessons guided you throughout your life?

_____

_____

_____

_____

_____

_____

Inner Teen

In what ways did you not feel safe or supported as a teen?

_____

_____

_____

_____

_____

_____

_____

_____

_____

_____

_____

_____

How did you handle your feelings about those experiences?

_____

_____

_____

_____

_____

_____

How did those experiences shape who you are today?

_____

_____

_____

_____

_____

_____

Parental Relations

What was your relationship with your parental guardians like during your teen years?

_____

_____

_____

_____

_____

_____

_____

_____

_____

_____

_____

_____

_____

Did you feel that your voice was heard? Did you feel safe to express your opinions and values?

_____

_____

_____

_____

_____

_____

Were you able to talk to your parental guardians about significant issues you were facing?

_____

_____

_____

_____

_____

_____

_____

Teen Adult

How is your inner teenager showing up in your life right now as an adult?

_____

_____

_____

_____

_____

_____

_____

_____

_____

_____

_____

_____

What does your inner teenager need from you right now?

_____

_____

_____

_____

_____

_____

What can you do to provide that for what your inner teenager needs from you right now?

_____

_____

_____

_____

_____

_____

_____

Anxiety

Describe all the things that make you feel anxious (people, places, situations, etc.).

_____

_____

_____

_____

_____

_____

_____

_____

_____

_____

_____

_____

_____

_____

Why do these things make you feel anxious?

_____

_____

_____

_____

_____

_____

How do you cope with anxiety? Is your anxiety holding
you back?

_____

_____

_____

_____

_____

_____

_____

@zenfulnote   Zenfulnote   DATE: /   /   /

Judgment

What do you judge about other people?

_____

_____

_____

_____

_____

_____

_____

_____

_____

_____

_____

_____

_____

_____

Do you engage in the same behaviors that you judge in other people?

_____

_____

_____

_____

_____

What do you judge yourself for?

_____

_____

_____

_____

_____

_____

Jealousy

Are there particular people or situations that trigger feelings of jealousy for you? What causes your jealousy to flare up?

_____

_____

_____

_____

_____

_____

_____

_____

_____

_____

_____

_____

_____

How often do you experience jealousy?

_____

_____

_____

_____

_____

What do you feel is at the root of your feelings of jealousy?

_____

_____

_____

_____

_____

_____

Being Jealous

Write about the most recent time you experienced feelings of jealousy.

_____

_____

_____

_____

_____

_____

_____

_____

_____

_____

_____

_____

_____

_____

_____

_____

_____

_____

Did you respond or react to the feelings of jealousy?
Did the jealousy bring up other feelings? If so, what were they?

_____

_____

_____

_____

_____

_____

Now, after reflecting, would you respond or react differently?

_____

_____

_____

_____

_____

_____

Managing Jealousy

How do you acknowledge jealous emotions?

_____

_____

_____

_____

_____

_____

_____

_____

_____

_____

_____

_____

_____

How do you manage your emotions when you experience jealousy?

_____

_____

_____

_____

_____

How would your life look if you shifted your jealousy into kindness?

_____

_____

_____

_____

_____

_____

@zenfulnote   Zenfulnote   DATE: / / /

Justifications

What is your definition of "justification"?

_____

_____

_____

_____

_____

_____

_____

_____

_____

_____

_____

_____

_____

_____

When do you think jealousy is not justified?

_____

_____

_____

_____

_____

When do you think jealousy is justified?

_____

_____

_____

_____

_____

_____

@zenfulnote   Zenfulnote   DATE: / / /

How does the feeling of jealousy affect how you see yourself?

_____

_____

_____

_____

_____

_____

_____

_____

_____

_____

_____

_____

How do you react when your jealous emotions occur?

_____

_____

_____

_____

_____

_____

How can you respond with kindness when your jealous
emotions occur?

_____

_____

_____

_____

_____

_____

Inspiration

Write down a time in your life when you felt a spark of inspiration or joy. Where were you? What were you doing? Who were you with?

_____

_____

_____

_____

_____

_____

_____

_____

_____

_____

_____

_____

_____

_____

_____

What inspired you most about that experience?

_____

_____

_____

_____

_____

How else can you express that same inspiration?

_____

_____

_____

_____

_____

_____

Compliments

What are the top three compliments others give you?

_____

_____

_____

_____

_____

_____

_____

_____

_____

_____

_____

_____

_____

_____

How do you feel when you receive these compliments?

_____

_____

_____

_____

_____

Do you believe that you embody those qualities?

_____

_____

_____

_____

_____

_____

Habits

What is the habit that you've been able to sustain the longest?

_____

_____

_____

_____

_____

_____

_____

_____

_____

_____

_____

_____

_____

What motivates you to keep this habit alive?

_____

_____

_____

_____

_____

Is there a part of you that would like to change this habit?

_____

_____

_____

_____

_____

_____

Accomplishments

Reflect on your past accomplishments in life: personal, physical, academic, spiritual, social, or anything else. Of all of these, which are you most proud of?

_____

_____

_____

_____

_____

_____

_____

_____

_____

_____

_____

_____

_____

_____

_____

_____

Why are you most proud of the accomplishments you listed?

How do your accomplishments motivate you?

What are your biggest dreams in life?

_____

_____

_____

_____

_____

_____

_____

_____

_____

_____

_____

_____

If your biggest dreams came true, what would you do?

_____

_____

_____

_____

_____

How would you feel?

_____

_____

_____

_____

_____

_____

Dream Life

Envision your dream life. How does it differ from your current life?

_____

_____

_____

_____

_____

_____

_____

_____

_____

_____

_____

_____

_____

What would your daily experience be like if you were living your dream life today?

_____

_____

_____

_____

_____

_____

What is holding you back from experiencing your dream life?

_____

_____

_____

_____

_____

_____

_____

Happiness

What makes you feel the happiest?

_____

_____

_____

_____

_____

_____

_____

_____

_____

_____

_____

_____

_____

_____

How can you experience happiness right now?

_____

_____

_____

_____

_____

_____

What can you do to bring more of that happiness into your
day-to-day life?

_____

_____

_____

_____

_____

_____

Freedom

What does freedom mean to you?

_____

_____

_____

_____

_____

_____

_____

_____

_____

_____

_____

_____

_____

_____

When do you feel most free?

_____

_____

_____

_____

_____

What is stopping you from experiencing freedom every day?

_____

_____

_____

_____

_____

_____

Envisioning Life

If you were living your dream life, what would that look like?

_____

_____

_____

_____

_____

_____

_____

_____

_____

_____

_____

_____

_____

How would you feel every day?

_____

_____

_____

_____

_____

What is the difference between your dream life versus
your current reality?

_____

_____

_____

_____

_____

_____

_____

Defining Moments

Reflect on your life experiences so far. What have been the defining moments or turning points?

_____

_____

_____

_____

_____

_____

_____

_____

_____

_____

_____

_____

_____

How did these pivotal moments make you feel?

_____

_____

_____

_____

_____

How did these turning points shape who you are today?

_____

_____

_____

_____

_____

_____

Making a Difference

What makes you feel like you are making a difference
in the world?

_____

_____

_____

_____

_____

_____

_____

_____

_____

_____

_____

_____

What actions do you take to allow yourself to make
a difference?

_____

_____

_____

_____

_____

How does it feel when you're making a difference?

_____

_____

_____

_____

_____

_____

Happy Day

Describe your happiest day. It could be a real memory, or your ideal, perfect day.

_____

_____

_____

_____

_____

_____

_____

_____

_____

_____

_____

_____

_____

_____

_____

_____

_____

What is it about this day that makes you feel happy?

_____

_____

_____

_____

_____

How often do you feel happy in your day-to-day life?

_____

_____

_____

_____

_____

_____

5

Get to
the Root

Come to this section whenever you are facing your shadows in real time.

Behaviors of your unconscious shadow include:

- Feeling angry, irritated, or anxious without a clear reason
- Blaming external factors for your problems, consistently playing the victim
- Ongoing negative thoughts and laziness
- Lack of motivation and doubting your capabilities
- Jealousy, negative thoughts toward others
- Feelings of guilt, shame

EXAMPLE

Getting to the Root of Your Shadow

Find a dim, quiet space to sit in. Tune in to your shadow.

What is triggering my shadow?   _My job and presentation tomorrow_

What thoughts am I having?   _I want to quit. This job sucks life_
from me. I can't do this presentation tomorrow, I don't feel prepared ...

What emotions am I experiencing?   _Anxiety, fear_

Close your eyes. Listen to your inner voice.
What three words come to your mind? Write them down.
They hold meaning.

Trapped	Nervous	Heavy

What memories or images come to mind when you focus
on these words? Connect with your inner child.

I think of a bird in a cage looking out from the inside. I know that
freedom exists on the other side, but I'm nervous to fly. I'm nervous and
anxious about my capabilities—what if I can't go far if I leave?
I feel heavy, and like something is weighing me down.
I felt like this as a child in school, always looking outside the window,
and struggling to understand the material in class.

Set the intention to energetically accept and love your inner
child. Let go.

Getting to the Root of Your Shadow

Find a dim, quiet space to sit in. Tune in to your shadow.

What is triggering my shadow? _____

What thoughts am I having? _____

_____

What emotions am I experiencing? _____

_____

Close your eyes. Listen to your inner voice.
What three words come to your mind? Write them down.
They hold meaning.

What memories or images come to mind when you focus
on these words? Connect with your inner child.

_____

_____

_____

_____

_____

_____

Set the intention to energetically accept and love your inner
child. Let go.

Getting to the Root of Your Shadow

Find a dim, quiet space to sit in. Tune in to your shadow.

What is triggering my shadow? _____

What thoughts am I having? _____

_____

What emotions am I experiencing? _____

_____

Close your eyes. Listen to your inner voice.
What three words come to your mind? Write them down.
They hold meaning.

What memories or images come to mind when you focus
on these words? Connect with your inner child.

_____

_____

_____

_____

_____

_____

Set the intention to energetically accept and love your inner
child. Let go.

Getting to the Root of Your Shadow

Find a dim, quiet space to sit in. Tune in to your shadow.

What is triggering my shadow? _____

What thoughts am I having? _____

_____

What emotions am I experiencing? _____

_____

Close your eyes. Listen to your inner voice.
What three words come to your mind? Write them down.
They hold meaning.

What memories or images come to mind when you focus
on these words? Connect with your inner child.

_____

_____

_____

_____

_____

_____

Set the intention to energetically accept and love your inner
child. Let go.

Getting to the Root of Your Shadow

Find a dim, quiet space to sit in. Tune in to your shadow.

What is triggering my shadow? _____

What thoughts am I having? _____

_____

What emotions am I experiencing? _____

_____

Close your eyes. Listen to your inner voice.
What three words come to your mind? Write them down.
They hold meaning.

What memories or images come to mind when you focus
on these words? Connect with your inner child.

_____

_____

_____

_____

_____

_____

Set the intention to energetically accept and love your inner
child. Let go.

Getting to the Root of Your Shadow

Find a dim, quiet space to sit in. Tune in to your shadow.

What is triggering my shadow? _____

What thoughts am I having? _____

_____

What emotions am I experiencing? _____

_____

Close your eyes. Listen to your inner voice.
What three words come to your mind? Write them down.
They hold meaning.

What memories or images come to mind when you focus
on these words? Connect with your inner child.

_____

_____

_____

_____

_____

_____

Set the intention to energetically accept and love your inner
child. Let go.

Getting to the Root of Your Shadow

Find a dim, quiet space to sit in. Tune in to your shadow.

What is triggering my shadow? _____

What thoughts am I having? _____

_____

What emotions am I experiencing? _____

_____

Close your eyes. Listen to your inner voice.
What three words come to your mind? Write them down.
They hold meaning.

What memories or images come to mind when you focus
on these words? Connect with your inner child.

_____

_____

_____

_____

_____

_____

Set the intention to energetically accept and love your inner
child. Let go.

Getting to the Root of Your Shadow

Find a dim, quiet space to sit in. Tune in to your shadow.

What is triggering my shadow? _____

What thoughts am I having? _____

_____

What emotions am I experiencing? _____

_____

Close your eyes. Listen to your inner voice.
What three words come to your mind? Write them down.
They hold meaning.

What memories or images come to mind when you focus
on these words? Connect with your inner child.

_____

_____

_____

_____

_____

_____

Set the intention to energetically accept and love your inner
child. Let go.

Getting to the Root of Your Shadow

Find a dim, quiet space to sit in. Tune in to your shadow.

What is triggering my shadow? _____

What thoughts am I having? _____

_____

What emotions am I experiencing? _____

_____

Close your eyes. Listen to your inner voice.
What three words come to your mind? Write them down.
They hold meaning.

What memories or images come to mind when you focus
on these words? Connect with your inner child.

_____

_____

_____

_____

_____

_____

Set the intention to energetically accept and love your inner
child. Let go.

Getting to the Root of Your Shadow

Find a dim, quiet space to sit in. Tune in to your shadow.

What is triggering my shadow? _____

What thoughts am I having? _____

_____

What emotions am I experiencing? _____

_____

Close your eyes. Listen to your inner voice.
What three words come to your mind? Write them down.
They hold meaning.

What memories or images come to mind when you focus
on these words? Connect with your inner child.

_____

_____

_____

_____

_____

_____

Set the intention to energetically accept and love your inner
child. Let go.

Getting to the Root of Your Shadow

Find a dim, quiet space to sit in. Tune in to your shadow.

What is triggering my shadow? _____

What thoughts am I having? _____

_____

What emotions am I experiencing? _____

_____

Close your eyes. Listen to your inner voice.
What three words come to your mind? Write them down.
They hold meaning.

What memories or images come to mind when you focus
on these words? Connect with your inner child.

_____

_____

_____

_____

_____

Set the intention to energetically accept and love your inner
child. Let go.

Getting to the Root of Your Shadow

Find a dim, quiet space to sit in. Tune in to your shadow.

What is triggering my shadow? _____

What thoughts am I having? _____
_____

What emotions am I experiencing? _____
_____

Close your eyes. Listen to your inner voice.
What three words come to your mind? Write them down.
They hold meaning.

What memories or images come to mind when you focus
on these words? Connect with your inner child.

_____
_____
_____
_____
_____

Set the intention to energetically accept and love your inner
child. Let go.

Getting to the Root of Your Shadow

Find a dim, quiet space to sit in. Tune in to your shadow.

What is triggering my shadow? _____

What thoughts am I having? _____
_____

What emotions am I experiencing? _____
_____

Close your eyes. Listen to your inner voice.
What three words come to your mind? Write them down.
They hold meaning.

What memories or images come to mind when you focus
on these words? Connect with your inner child.

_____

_____

_____

_____

_____

Set the intention to energetically accept and love your inner
child. Let go.

Getting to the Root of Your Shadow

Find a dim, quiet space to sit in. Tune in to your shadow.

What is triggering my shadow? _____

What thoughts am I having? _____
_____

What emotions am I experiencing? _____
_____

Close your eyes. Listen to your inner voice.
What three words come to your mind? Write them down.
They hold meaning.

What memories or images come to mind when you focus
on these words? Connect with your inner child.

_____
_____
_____
_____
_____
_____

Set the intention to energetically accept and love your inner
child. Let go.

Getting to the Root of Your Shadow

Find a dim, quiet space to sit in. Tune in to your shadow.

What is triggering my shadow? _____

What thoughts am I having? _____

_____

What emotions am I experiencing? _____

_____

Close your eyes. Listen to your inner voice.
What three words come to your mind? Write them down.
They hold meaning.

What memories or images come to mind when you focus
on these words? Connect with your inner child.

_____

_____

_____

_____

_____

_____

Set the intention to energetically accept and love your inner
child. Let go.

Getting to the Root of Your Shadow

Find a dim, quiet space to sit in. Tune in to your shadow.

What is triggering my shadow? _____

What thoughts am I having? _____
_____

What emotions am I experiencing? _____
_____

Close your eyes. Listen to your inner voice.
What three words come to your mind? Write them down.
They hold meaning.

What memories or images come to mind when you focus
on these words? Connect with your inner child.

_____
_____
_____
_____
_____
_____

Set the intention to energetically accept and love your inner
child. Let go.

Getting to the Root of Your Shadow

Find a dim, quiet space to sit in. Tune in to your shadow.

What is triggering my shadow? _____

What thoughts am I having? _____

_____

What emotions am I experiencing? _____

_____

Close your eyes. Listen to your inner voice.
What three words come to your mind? Write them down.
They hold meaning.

What memories or images come to mind when you focus
on these words? Connect with your inner child.

_____

_____

_____

_____

_____

_____

Set the intention to energetically accept and love your inner
child. Let go.

Getting to the Root of Your Shadow

Find a dim, quiet space to sit in. Tune in to your shadow.

What is triggering my shadow? _____

What thoughts am I having? _____
_____

What emotions am I experiencing? _____
_____

Close your eyes. Listen to your inner voice.
What three words come to your mind? Write them down.
They hold meaning.

What memories or images come to mind when you focus
on these words? Connect with your inner child.

_____
_____
_____
_____
_____
_____

Set the intention to energetically accept and love your inner
child. Let go.

Getting to the Root of Your Shadow

Find a dim, quiet space to sit in. Tune in to your shadow.

What is triggering my shadow? _____

What thoughts am I having? _____
_____

What emotions am I experiencing? _____
_____

Close your eyes. Listen to your inner voice.
What three words come to your mind? Write them down.
They hold meaning.

What memories or images come to mind when you focus
on these words? Connect with your inner child.

_____

_____

_____

_____

_____

_____

Set the intention to energetically accept and love your inner
child. Let go.

Getting to the Root of Your Shadow

Find a dim, quiet space to sit in. Tune in to your shadow.

What is triggering my shadow? _____

What thoughts am I having? _____

_____

What emotions am I experiencing? _____

_____

Close your eyes. Listen to your inner voice.
What three words come to your mind? Write them down.
They hold meaning.

What memories or images come to mind when you focus
on these words? Connect with your inner child.

_____

_____

_____

_____

_____

Set the intention to energetically accept and love your inner
child. Let go.

Getting to the Root of Your Shadow

Find a dim, quiet space to sit in. Tune in to your shadow.

What is triggering my shadow? _____

What thoughts am I having? _____

_____

What emotions am I experiencing? _____

_____

Close your eyes. Listen to your inner voice.
What three words come to your mind? Write them down.
They hold meaning.

What memories or images come to mind when you focus
on these words? Connect with your inner child.

_____

_____

_____

_____

_____

_____

Set the intention to energetically accept and love your inner
child. Let go.

Getting to the Root of Your Shadow

Find a dim, quiet space to sit in. Tune in to your shadow.

What is triggering my shadow? _____

What thoughts am I having? _____

_____

What emotions am I experiencing? _____

_____

Close your eyes. Listen to your inner voice.
What three words come to your mind? Write them down.
They hold meaning.

What memories or images come to mind when you focus
on these words? Connect with your inner child.

_____

_____

_____

_____

_____

_____

Set the intention to energetically accept and love your inner
child. Let go.

Getting to the Root of Your Shadow

Find a dim, quiet space to sit in. Tune in to your shadow.

What is triggering my shadow? _____

What thoughts am I having? _____

_____

What emotions am I experiencing? _____

_____

Close your eyes. Listen to your inner voice.
What three words come to your mind? Write them down.
They hold meaning.

What memories or images come to mind when you focus
on these words? Connect with your inner child.

_____

_____

_____

_____

_____

_____

Set the intention to energetically accept and love your inner
child. Let go.

Getting to the Root of Your Shadow

Find a dim, quiet space to sit in. Tune in to your shadow.

What is triggering my shadow? _____

What thoughts am I having? _____
_____

What emotions am I experiencing? _____
_____

Close your eyes. Listen to your inner voice.
What three words come to your mind? Write them down.
They hold meaning.

What memories or images come to mind when you focus
on these words? Connect with your inner child.

_____
_____
_____
_____
_____

Set the intention to energetically accept and love your inner
child. Let go.

Getting to the Root of Your Shadow

Find a dim, quiet space to sit in. Tune in to your shadow.

What is triggering my shadow? _____

What thoughts am I having? _____

_____

What emotions am I experiencing? _____

_____

Close your eyes. Listen to your inner voice.
What three words come to your mind? Write them down.
They hold meaning.

What memories or images come to mind when you focus
on these words? Connect with your inner child.

_____

_____

_____

_____

_____

_____

Set the intention to energetically accept and love your inner
child. Let go.

Getting to the Root of Your Shadow

Find a dim, quiet space to sit in. Tune in to your shadow.

What is triggering my shadow? _____

What thoughts am I having? _____

_____

What emotions am I experiencing? _____

_____

Close your eyes. Listen to your inner voice.
What three words come to your mind? Write them down.
They hold meaning.

What memories or images come to mind when you focus
on these words? Connect with your inner child.

_____

_____

_____

_____

_____

_____

Set the intention to energetically accept and love your inner
child. Let go.

Getting to the Root of Your Shadow

Find a dim, quiet space to sit in. Tune in to your shadow.

What is triggering my shadow? _____

What thoughts am I having? _____

_____

What emotions am I experiencing? _____

_____

Close your eyes. Listen to your inner voice.
What three words come to your mind? Write them down.
They hold meaning.

What memories or images come to mind when you focus
on these words? Connect with your inner child.

_____

_____

_____

_____

_____

_____

Set the intention to energetically accept and love your inner
child. Let go.

Getting to the Root of Your Shadow

Find a dim, quiet space to sit in. Tune in to your shadow.

What is triggering my shadow? _____

What thoughts am I having? _____

_____

What emotions am I experiencing? _____

_____

Close your eyes. Listen to your inner voice.
What three words come to your mind? Write them down.
They hold meaning.

What memories or images come to mind when you focus
on these words? Connect with your inner child.

_____

_____

_____

_____

_____

_____

Set the intention to energetically accept and love your inner
child. Let go.

Getting to the Root of Your Shadow

Find a dim, quiet space to sit in. Tune in to your shadow.

What is triggering my shadow? _____

What thoughts am I having? _____

_____

What emotions am I experiencing? _____

_____

Close your eyes. Listen to your inner voice.
What three words come to your mind? Write them down.
They hold meaning.

What memories or images come to mind when you focus
on these words? Connect with your inner child.

_____

_____

_____

_____

_____

_____

Set the intention to energetically accept and love your inner
child. Let go.

Getting to the Root of Your Shadow

Find a dim, quiet space to sit in. Tune in to your shadow.

What is triggering my shadow? _____

What thoughts am I having? _____
_____

What emotions am I experiencing? _____
_____

Close your eyes. Listen to your inner voice.
What three words come to your mind? Write them down.
They hold meaning.

What memories or images come to mind when you focus
on these words? Connect with your inner child.

_____

_____

_____

_____

_____

_____

Set the intention to energetically accept and love your inner
child. Let go.

Getting to the Root of Your Shadow

Find a dim, quiet space to sit in. Tune in to your shadow.

What is triggering my shadow? _____

What thoughts am I having? _____

_____

What emotions am I experiencing? _____

_____

Close your eyes. Listen to your inner voice.
What three words come to your mind? Write them down.
They hold meaning.

What memories or images come to mind when you focus
on these words? Connect with your inner child.

_____

_____

_____

_____

_____

Set the intention to energetically accept and love your inner
child. Let go.

Getting to the Root of Your Shadow

Find a dim, quiet space to sit in. Tune in to your shadow.

What is triggering my shadow? _____

What thoughts am I having? _____

_____

What emotions am I experiencing? _____

_____

Close your eyes. Listen to your inner voice.
What three words come to your mind? Write them down.
They hold meaning.

What memories or images come to mind when you focus
on these words? Connect with your inner child.

_____

_____

_____

_____

_____

Set the intention to energetically accept and love your inner
child. Let go.

Getting to the Root of Your Shadow

Find a dim, quiet space to sit in. Tune in to your shadow.

What is triggering my shadow? _____

What thoughts am I having? _____
_____

What emotions am I experiencing? _____
_____

Close your eyes. Listen to your inner voice.
What three words come to your mind? Write them down.
They hold meaning.

What memories or images come to mind when you focus
on these words? Connect with your inner child.

_____
_____
_____
_____
_____
_____

Set the intention to energetically accept and love your inner
child. Let go.

Getting to the Root of Your Shadow

Find a dim, quiet space to sit in. Tune in to your shadow.

What is triggering my shadow? _____

What thoughts am I having? _____

_____

What emotions am I experiencing? _____

_____

Close your eyes. Listen to your inner voice.
What three words come to your mind? Write them down.
They hold meaning.

What memories or images come to mind when you focus
on these words? Connect with your inner child.

_____

_____

_____

_____

_____

_____

Set the intention to energetically accept and love your inner
child. Let go.

Getting to the Root of Your Shadow

Find a dim, quiet space to sit in. Tune in to your shadow.

What is triggering my shadow? _____

What thoughts am I having? _____

_____

What emotions am I experiencing? _____

_____

Close your eyes. Listen to your inner voice.
What three words come to your mind? Write them down.
They hold meaning.

What memories or images come to mind when you focus
on these words? Connect with your inner child.

_____

_____

_____

_____

_____

_____

Set the intention to energetically accept and love your inner
child. Let go.

Getting to the Root of Your Shadow

Find a dim, quiet space to sit in. Tune in to your shadow.

What is triggering my shadow? _____

What thoughts am I having? _____
_____

What emotions am I experiencing? _____
_____

Close your eyes. Listen to your inner voice.
What three words come to your mind? Write them down.
They hold meaning.

What memories or images come to mind when you focus
on these words? Connect with your inner child.

_____
_____
_____
_____
_____

Set the intention to energetically accept and love your inner
child. Let go.

Resources

- Zenfulnote App—This is an app that allows you to track emotional triggers, glimmers, and moods. It is a virtual space for self-exploration with prompts, exercises, and learning materials around self-healing and shadow work.

- National Institute of Mental Health (NIMH)—This is a government-funded organization that provides information and resources on various mental health conditions.

- American Psychological Association (APA)—This is a professional organization for psychologists that offers information and resources for both mental health professionals and the general public.

- Psychology Today (Psychologytoday.com/us)—This is a directory website that allows you to search by location and provider type for therapists, psychologists, and more.

- National Alliance on Mental Illness (NAMI)—This is a grassroots organization that provides support, education, and advocacy for people living with mental health conditions.

- Depression and Bipolar Support Alliance (DBSA)—This is a national organization that provides peer support, education, and advocacy for people living with depression and bipolar disorder.

- The Depression Project—This is an online platform that provides resources, support, and a community for people living with depression.

- Therapy for Black Girls—This is an online directory and resource that helps Black women with support from licensed mental health providers.

- Therapy for LatinX—This is a database of therapists who either identify as LatinX or have worked closely with LatinX communities and understand their needs. www.therapyforlatinx.com

- Talkspace—An online therapy service that offers support to individuals dealing with depression, anxiety, and a wide range of mental health issues, facilitating access to professional counseling.

- BetterHelp—A digital counseling platform that connects users with therapists for personalized treatment of depression, stress, and other psychological concerns, enhancing mental wellness.

- Anxiety and Depression Association of America (ADDA)—This is a nonprofit organization that provides education, support, and advocacy for people living with anxiety, depression, and other related disorders.

- Advanced Healing Wellness Center (AHWC)—This is a center that emphasizes a holistic approach to health and wellness. Its approach integrates physical, emotional, mental, nutritional, and spiritual components and restores balance inwardly and outwardly.

DOWNLOAD
the APP

Scan Here

WHERE TECHNOLOGY MEETS
INNER TRANSFORMATION

• Track Triggers

• Check In with Feelings

• Journal Prompts

• Healing Exercises

• View Emotional Patterns over Time